IT'S TIME TO EAT BARBECUE

It's Time to Eat
BARBECUE

Walter the Educator

Silent King Books
A WhichHead Entertainment Imprint

Copyright © 2024 by Walter the Educator

All rights reserved. No part of this book may be reproduced in any manner whatsoever without written per- mission except in the case of brief quotations embodied in critical articles and reviews.

First Printing, 2024

Disclaimer

This book is a literary work; the story is not about specific persons, locations, situations, and/or circumstances unless mentioned in a historical context. Any resemblance to real persons, locations, situations, and/or circumstances is coincidental. This book is for entertainment and informational purposes only. The author and publisher offer this information without warranties expressed or implied. No matter the grounds, neither the author nor the publisher will be accountable for any losses, injuries, or other damages caused by the reader's use of this book. The use of this book acknowledges an understanding and acceptance of this disclaimer.

It's Time to Eat BARBECUE is a collectible early learning book by Walter the Educator suitable for all ages belonging to Walter the Educator's Time to Eat Book Series. Collect more books at WaltertheEducator.com

USE THE EXTRA SPACE TO TAKE NOTES AND DOCUMENT YOUR MEMORIES

BARBECUE

The sun is shining, the grill is hot,

It's Time to Eat
Barbecue

It's barbecue time, ready or not!

The smoky smell drifts through the air,

A feast is coming, we'll all share.

Burgers sizzle with a happy sound,

Juicy patties, big and round.

Hot dogs dance with a fiery glow,

Wrapped in buns, they steal the show.

Chicken wings with a saucy coat,

Tender bites that make us gloat.

Ribs so sticky, sweet, and bold,

A barbecue treasure worth more than gold.

Corn on the cob with golden specks,

Butter dripping down its necks.

Veggies grilled with charred delight,

Bright and tasty, a healthy bite.

It's Time to Eat
Barbecue

Barbecue sauce, tangy and sweet,

Drizzled on top, it's the final treat.

Smoky flavors in every bite,

Turning lunch into pure delight.

The picnic table is where we meet,

Friends and family, all to eat.

Laughter rings as we pass the plate,

Barbecue time is truly great.

Don't forget sides like coleslaw crunch,

Beans and bread to finish our lunch.

Watermelon slices cool and bright,

Make barbecue time feel just right.

The sun dips low, the sky turns red,

But barbecue dreams fill our head.

It's Time to Eat
Barbecue

A meal so joyful, it's easy to see,

Barbecue time is the place to be!

So grab your fork, come take a seat,

Barbecue's here, it's time to eat!

A smoky, savory, tasty affair,

Barbecue love is beyond compare!

Marshmallows toast as the fire glows,

A sweet little treat as the evening slows.

Barbecue magic, a day to recall,

It's Time to Eat
Barbecue

The best kind of feast to share with all!

ABOUT THE CREATOR

Walter the Educator is one of the pseudonyms for Walter Anderson. Formally educated in Chemistry, Business, and Education, he is an educator, an author, a diverse entrepreneur, and he is the son of a disabled war veteran. "Walter the Educator" shares his time between educating and creating. He holds interests and owns several creative projects that entertain, enlighten, enhance, and educate, hoping to inspire and motivate you. Follow, find new works, and stay up to date with Walter the Educator™

at WaltertheEducator.com

www.ingramcontent.com/pod-product-compliance
Lightning Source LLC
LaVergne TN
LVHW052010060526
838201LV00059B/3957